Catch the Wave

A Self- Publishing Workshop

There are many routes to publication – use these basic resources
to prepare, research, and get current with the industry.

Isinglass Press
SILVERLAKE, WASHINGTON

Isinglass Press
PO Box 1731
Castle Rock, WA 98611
www.isinglasspress.com

Publisher's Note: This product is meant for educational purposes only. Names, characters, places, and incidents are presented by the author without intent to defame. The opinions expressed herein are those of the author and not necessarily attributed to any other. All comments related to any work presented in this section should be directed to the author.

Cover Design by www.Humblenations.com
Interior Design by www.BookDesignTemplates.com

Ordering Information:
Quantity sales. Special discounts are available on quantity purchases by corporations, associations, and others. For details, contact the "Special Sales Department" at the address above.

Catch the Wave: A Self-Publishing Workshop / Lesann Berry. -- 1st ed.
ISBN 978-1-939316-08-0

Table of Contents

PART ONE

Know the Terms

The only constant in e-book publishing is how fast things change.

❧

T rying to sort through all the information about self-publishing can be daunting. The sheer volume of anecdotal experience is overwhelming and makes it difficult to differentiate quality information from data that is no longer pertinent.

Like any industry, publishing tosses around buzz words for which there are multiple definitions. The more informed you become about the options available, the best choices you can make when it comes to your own publishing process. Most of the terminology doesn't make much difference for our purposes, but some clarification may be helpful.

So, what is the main distinction between the traditional and self-publishing paths?

Traditional Publishing refers to the publishing model where a writer completes a manuscript, queries until they retain an agent, and then the agent submits the author's work to various contacts at publishing houses. Today, this is also referred to as the Agency Model or Legacy Publishing.

Self-Publishing differs in that the author is also the publisher, responsible for preparing the manuscript for publication and taking on the role of distribution and marketing. In today's marketplace this is also called Indie Publishing.

Both are good methods with different pros and cons. Choose the approach that best fits your goals.

Is self-publishing the right choice for you?

Evaluate your reasons for considering the idea in the first place and be realistic with your answers.

1. Do you want to simply have your work printed?
2. Do you care if nobody else ever reads it?
3. Do you want to share your work with strangers?
4. Do you want to produce income with your writing?
5. Do you have the skills to write, edit, and market?
6. If not, are you willing to pay others?

If you just want a published book to hold while you dance around the room – then self-publishing offers you that chance. This is an especially awesome opportunity for folks who have a book they want to produce for their friends and family. Children's stories, genealogical resources, and cookbooks filled with treasured recipes are excellent for this publishing path – simply because most aren't viewed from the standpoint of being commercial endeavors. You never know, one of them might turn out to be a hit, but you go into the process knowing that isn't your primary motivation.

The perception that self-publishing success is the result of a few simple actions is false. A small percentage of the people who submit their polished work to agents get offers of representation. An even smaller percentage of those authors find long-term success in publishing. A minute fraction of that percentage hit the best-seller lists.

Indie Publishing is equally challenging. There are only a small percentage of successful self-published authors on the best-seller lists. Most self-published books sell less than 500 copies, primarily because no one knows they exist.

Don't set yourself up for disappointment. If you plan to self-publish your work with the goal of making a pile of money, it might happen, but it probably won't. Recognize this fact from the beginning. Looking at the long-tail approach to self-pubbing provides a more realistic view.

There are no shortcuts to success.

Many midlist authors make a successful living but they work hard to be successful. There are more hybrid authors today than ever before – these are traditionally published writers who also self-publish or have taken back the rights on their older works and re-released them to a newly energized and polarized marketplace.

How do you get started?

First, you have to write a good book. Second, you have to pay for editing. Maybe twice. Third, you have to purchase or have a nice cover designed by someone who understands what a book cover needs to do in a digital market. Then you have to get your work in the hands of your readers. Do you know who they are and how to reach them?

Jane Friedman, a former editor with Writer's Digest and a publishing expert, offers many helpful resources on her website (www.janefriedman.com). She offers some of the best insights to modern publishing. The following list of questions was posed by Orna Ross, the director of the Alliance for Independent Authors, and is discussed in-depth at the web address listed at the end. This succinct summation might help you decide if self-publishing is the correct choice for you. Welcome to the new paradigm.5

1. Are you positive and proactive?
2. Are you brave?
3. Are you hardworking?
4. Are you entrepreneurial?
5. Are you resilient?
6. Do you base decisions on research?
7. Do you have good financial sense?
8. Are you collaborative and supportive?
9. Have you tried to find an agent or publisher?
10. Have you made a plan for copyediting, formatting, cover design, and ISBNs?
11. Have you thought about your team?
12. Do you understand your niche?
13. Do you know who your reader is?
14. Do you have a marketing plan – a plan to reach readers?
15. Have you made a plan for your next book?

Don't forget to check out this link:

http://janefriedman.com/2013/05/17/should-you-self-publish/

PART TWO

Listen to the Experts

What you need to know is determined by what you want to do.

❦

Rather than repeat what other people have already said with great eloquence, I've included some recommended reading in this section that will help interested self-publishers navigate the pitfalls of the process. You don't have to do it all yourself. But, anything you don't undertake as a DIY project, means you'll be coughing up the cash to pay someone else for their time and expertise. Sometimes that's the best way to go. There is no substitution for knowledge about the industry. As a professional, you want to know how everything works and what you should monitor for important changes.

Use the links in this part to benefit from the full discussion on the websites – and remember that the comments are filled with excellent suggestions and experiences, many from people who are helping to define this new era in publishing. Ferret out the information and approaches that best work for you and tweak them until the fit is comfortable. Just as in writing, there are no real rules.

Learn about self-publishing:

Five Things Beginners Need to Know about Ebook Publishing
http://janefriedman.com/2011/08/09/5-things-beginners-need-to-know-about-e-book-publishing/

The Basics of DIY Ebook Publishing
http://www.writersdigest.com/online-editor/the-basics-of-diy-e-book-publishing

How to Self-Publish an Ebook
http://reviews.cnet.com/8301-18438_7-20010547-82/how-to-self-publish-an-ebook/

10 Questions to Ask Any E-publishing Service
http://janefriedman.com/2012/02/10/10-questions-epublishing/

How to Make Money on Ebooks
http://jakonrath.blogspot.com/2010/07/how-to-make-money-on-ebooks.html

A Million Self-Published Books
http://www.copyblogger.com/cj-lyons-entreproducer/

5 Things I've Learned from Self-Publishing
http://jamescalbraith.quora.com/5-Things-Ive-learned-from-self-publishing

Things change incredibly fast as the publishing world navigates new technology – be prepared for ups and downs. It's a work in progress. Identifying the experts can be tough, so here's a list of people who have been in the trenches and can offer their experience as well as their insights when it comes to riding the publishing wave.

Stay current with publishing news:

Jane Friedman
http://janefriedman.com/

Dean Wesley Smith
http://www.deanwesleysmith.com/

J.A. Konrath
http://www.jakonrath.com/

Joanna Penn
http://joannapenn.com/

Self-Publishing Podcast
http://selfpublishingpodcast.com/

Joel Friedlander
http://www.thebookdesigner.com/

David Gaughgran
http://davidgaughran.wordpress.com/

Guy Kawasaki

http://www.guykawasaki.com/

The Passive Voice

http://www.thepassivevoice.com/

Kristine Rusch

http://www.kristinekathrynrusch.com/

Bob Mayer

http://www.bobmayer.org/

The Shatzkin Files

http://www.idealog.com/blog/

Future Book

http://futurebook.net/

Digital Book World

http://www.digitalbookworld.com/

Many of these sites offer downloadable guides to self-publishing if you sign up for their email newsletters. I recommend you do. Collective experience is there for the taking. The more guidance from people who know how to do it right, the better your experience in self-publishing will prove.

Sites like the Kindle Boards (http://www.kboards.com/) feature the helpful ears and eyes of people who have been in your shoes. It never hurts to read the publishing guides and formatting information available at *every* outlet. Sometimes the tiniest bit of advice makes all the difference. Use all the available resources you can find.

Form your own team of industry-savvy people. Create connections to other authors. Form coalitions of professionals who are willing to share information. The more we know about what works and what doesn't, the better prepared we are to harness the power of reaching the reading public. Make a forum on Facebook or Google+ so you can chat and post and share as colleagues. Use your network to create a strong collective base of information.

Avoid turning your affiliates into a mutual admiration society. Don't swap false reviews or try to "game the system" in dumb ways – that defeats the purpose of sharing what really works.

Authors who create strong fan-bases often develop what are called street teams. This is another idea borrowed from other industries. These are fans and supporters who take over some of the work of promotion and representation on your behalf. They publicize appearances and upcoming book releases, offering their expertise in pertinent areas. They want to see you succeed. They become vested in your work. Of course, you have to keep an eye open to make sure the focus stays where you want it aimed.

The self-publishing path requires many steps – get started!

PART THREE

Use Available Tools

Your goal is to produce the absolutely best product you can.

T he cumulative amount of information available to the interested self-publisher increases steadily over time. Some of these tools are more helpful than others, but you may find yourself in need a resource that someone else understands intuitively. Outside of writing the book itself, you can outsource all of your publishing needs if you choose – but make sure you understand the risks inherent in turning over your word-baby to strangers.

Remember that you are jumping into an industry where the bottom line is the same as in any other business endeavor. Money talks and there are a lot of people out there trying to make a living off writers who aren't making one. Invest your time wisely. Make informed decisions.

Don't waste your words.

I've included a list of tools you might find valuable for creating a digital book, but first, let's talk about formatting files. While you write your story in whatever format you prefer, things get more complicated when it comes time to upload your book to a retailer. There are many different formats and it seems like everyone has a different preference. In some cases you send your manuscript through a program that works like an old-fashioned meat grinder, chewing up and formatting your novel to fit the system requirements. Results vary. Sometimes the finished file transfer is perfect the first time through – but other times, for inexplicable reasons, the process derails and must be repeated.

Here's a quick list of common file type formats:

1. MOBI (used for KINDLE)
2. EPUB (used for iBOOKS, KOBO, and others)
3. BBeB (older format used by SONY)
3. PDF (primarily for upload use)

There are dozens of other file types but EPUB has become the international standard for most reading devices. In gernal, the more proprietary the program, the smaller the library the retailer offers to consumers – although this certainly doesn't apply to Amazon. Should you need to translate a file from one format to another, search the web for a conversion site. I use ZAMZAR (http://www.zamzar.com/) when I need to convert a file because they have a FREE option.

People who design print books and work in publishing spend a lot of money to purchase programs like InDesign and Adobe Photoshop so they can fine-tune the layout and do file conversions as needed. The casual self-publisher doesn't need to do this unless they choose to (Adobe offers a monthly rate fee which makes this much more cost-effective). There are also numerous FREE programs that offer similar results – just plan on committing some time to the process if you aren't already familiar with such software programs. The learning curve can be high. This is one reason for the growth of a support industry around Indie Publishing. There are businesses that format for you, even uploading to various outlets, if you're willing to pay a fee. This offers less work for you but you'll pay every time you want to make a change unless they offer a subscription rate.

The more you can do yourself, the less expense is incurred. When your goal is to produce a quality product, you want to consider if outsourcing is the best choice, despite the cost. You can save a few bucks here and there and produce something that looks homespun – which is fine – as long as you aren't trying to compete in a marketplace (which you are). The accessibility of some of the following resources depends on whether you use Apple or PC for your computer needs.

Resources for formatting:

Calibre (a FREE conversion tool)
http://calibre-ebook.com/

Sigil (a FREE formatting tool – more technical)
https://code.google.com/p/sigil/

Press Books (a FREE formatting tool)
http://pressbooks.com/

Apple iBooks Author (exclusive to the Apple iBookstore)
http://www.apple.com/ibooks-author/

Scrivener (formatting and conversion tool)
http://www.literatureandlatte.com/scrivener.php

AerBook Maker (good for multimedia-driven work)
http://aerbook.com/site/

Apple Pages (formatting and conversion tool)
http://www.apple.com/iwork/pages/

E-book Creation: A Guide for Writers (superb downloads)
http://www.ljcohen.net/downloads.html#ebook

GIMP (a FREE alternative to Photoshop)
http://www.gimp.org/

Software provides many tools to assist authors in writing and creating quality products, but there are other types of tools that can be and should be utilized: primarily social media and websites/blogs. The ultimate goal of having a presence on the internet is so interested readers and fans can find you.

Do I need a social media presence?

Yes.

Much has been made of the importance and value of interacting on social media. Having a blog for authors to promote themselves through web venues is proffered as essential to success. My advice is to use the formats that appeal to you and ignore the rest. There is no magical formula that leads to the desired result. Despite the rhetoric surrounding the importance of Facebook "likes" and "followers" on this platform or that social media...none of it has value unless the interaction is genuine.

Statistics don't always translate into sales – and remember, we're interested in moving our books.

Ten active readers who follow your blog, leaving comments on your posts and engaging in personal interaction, is better than 10,000 hits a month from search engines and spambots who are attracted by keyword stuffing. Dedicated readers who are interested in your next release are far more useful to you as an author than five hundred random people who push the "like" button on a social media profile.

People who are interested in what you have to say are more likely to buy and read your book. More importantly, they are far more likely to tell a friend or recommend your work to others – that's how a fan base is built.

Make social media fun for you. Look at the advice other people offer but make your own determination. Learn what works for your personality, your time and schedule, and your goals. Lots of people enjoy dictating how a specific platform should be used, but that doesn't mean they're correct. There are many social media platforms. Below is a list of the social media I use – with links on my blog (www.lesannberry.com) so people can simply click and follow, if they feel so inclined.

Twitter
https://twitter.com/

Triberr
http://triberr.com/

Google +
https://plus.google.com/

Goodreads
http://www.goodreads.com/

Facebook
https://www.facebook.com/

Pinterest
http://pinterest.com/

A simple internet search will produce tutorials for best practices and plenty of anecdotal input about people's success rates in using each platform for connecting with and/or marketing their work. This is a somewhat contentious issue because social media is used differently by people and depending on your focus, the way others use it may grate. While there are numerous other sites, these are currently the most active ones.

Do I need a website or a blog?

Yes.

Make a website so people can find you if they go looking. You can say they won't, but somebody will. Do you need both a blog and a website? Only if you want to have both. A static website filled with your author information is important. If you want to blog about whatever interests you, please do. Again, despite what the rhetoric suggests, if you don't want to blog – you needn't. It really is that easy.

Don't invest in expensive professional web design. Unless you have a free acolyte to pressure into service, you can create a gorgeous simple website using a blog platform like Wordpress or Blogger in a single afternoon. The beauty of this approach is how simple and beautiful the results are and you remain in control. Tweak the site and content any time you feel like it – it's all FREE.

If you like the idea but aren't thrilled by the idea of having a website address that reads like www.yourname.wordpress.com –

then you can personalize your FREE website/blog with your own purchased domain name for $26/year (this is for a private registration listing).

In case you aren't familiar with blogging platforms – it's essentially a website template that is hosted somewhere else that you can fill out with your information. They're used by millions of individuals and businesses, offering instant web accessibility and professional results for FREE. Two of the largest platforms are Wordpress and Blogger. I've used both and each offers lots of bells and whistles. Google owns Blogger and is likely to be around for a long time to come, but if I had to recommend one over the other, I would suggest Wordpress.

The reason for this is simple, WP is open-source and in constant development. Something that often confuses newcomers is the fact that two different types of platform (.com and .org) are offered through Wordpress. The main difference is that wordpress.com is FREE and hosted by the people who run Wordpress – whereas wordpress.org is also FREE but you have to pay to host the files somewhere. The .org option also allows you to install and use an endless supply of plug-ins and widgets – which is something you probably don't really need in the beginning. Start simple.

Blogging Platforms
http://wordpress.com/
http://wordpress.org/
http://www.blogger.com/

While there is a glut of information on the internet, I have several suggested sites that offer great instructions and insights to blogging. You want to make it meaningful for both you and the audience. ProBlogger is excellent – their archives offer answers to virtually every blog-related question ever asked.

Blogging requires commitment and eats up writing time. Consistency is important or your readers won't know when to stop and visit. A successful blog provides a rich environment to engage with others but it isn't the only method for doing so. One thing a blog offers is regular writing practice and a venue to connect personal interests to your professional life in an entirely new way.

Resources if you're thinking about blogging:

How to Blog: Blogging Tips for Beginners
http://www.problogger.net/archives/2006/02/14/blogging-for-beginners-2/

Get Started Guide: Blogging for Writers
http://janefriedman.com/2011/08/24/blogging-for-writers/

The Top Ten Blogs for Writers
http://www.copyblogger.com/the-top-10-blogs-for-writers/

A Beginner's Guide for Authors
http://annerallen.blogspot.com/2011/12/how-to-blog-beginners-guide-for-authors.html

Should I start an email list?

Yes.

I know it feels premature but this is really one of the best ways to accumulate a mailing list of people who want to hear from you. Nobody likes to be spammed, right? If you begin collecting the email addresses of people who are vested in your success from the beginning, you will be way ahead of most established authors. Again, it isn't quantity but quality that matters.

Don't spam people. Send a newsletter when you really have something to share. You can offer something to entice people to join (a lot of authors give away stories and how-to-guides). Limit the amount of self-promotion and offer useful content that your readers will appreciate. Keep in mind that the public and the law define spam in different ways. You can harvest subscribers from your website but I recommend using a service like Mailchimp which is FREE. They have a nice plug-in that you can host on your website where people can subscribe directly to the mailing list. If you want, you can sign up to my mailing list at www.lesannberry.com to give it a try (yes, this is self-serving). Mailchimp provides lots of metrics that help you to figure out if your efforts are working. They also feature an easy way for people to unsubscribe if they choose- which is important to obey spam laws.

A note about branding:

The idea of branding is touted as an essential part of author identity. Consider this a work in progress because you are your brand and that persona will grow and change just as your writing will. Branding helps you identify your audience and the criteria that appeals to those folks. Great brands are instantly recognizable.

Think of well-known people and products.

Consistency is helpful, as is being able to change with the market. Not only do you want to keep the interest of current readers, you also want to continue increasing your appeal to new ones. Consider your brand in all aspects of your work. Is your brand reflected in your book covers, your titles, the fonts and art concepts of your website and marketing materials? Keep your brand consistent in these areas and you will be uniquely recognizable.

When the time comes to brainstorm and identify how to market yourself as a brand, do a lot of reading. Figure out how you want others to perceive you. Use keywords like "brand" and "platform" combined with "author" and "publishing" to ferret out information that is specific to your needs. People with experience in these areas understand the value of perception but they don't always comprehend the needs of an author who will not be writing the same product every time. Here are a few sites that provide some context for the concerns in building an author brand identity and a platform:

A Definition of Author Platform
http://janefriedman.com/2012/03/13/author-platform-definition/

Understanding Author Platform
http://warriorwriters.wordpress.com/2013/01/16/the-most-powerful-social-media-tool-for-building-an-author-platform-part-1/

What is an Author Platform and Why do You Need One Now?
http://www.thecreativepenn.com/2009/06/26/author-platform/

How to Discover and Build Your Author Brand
http://www.thecreativepenn.com/2009/08/03/how-to-discover-and-build-your-author-brand/

PART FOUR

Covers are Critical

Your book cover is the first taste a reader gets of your work.

❧

Book covers are important. They offer a visual tease about the contents wrapped inside the package. Fiction readers are savvy about extrapolating the genre or type of story from a cover – the wrong look can cost you readers. A poor cover design wastes your hard work. And, it is an unnecessary risk in today's market.

Most self-published authors do not have the option to see their books sitting on the shelves of a local bookstore. There is no expectation of an audience browsing the stacks and being attracted to your beautiful multicolor cover. They can't pick up your book and admire the smooth glossy images or open it up and smell the interior. They can't flip through the pages or sample the wares.

A book cover has to do several things. First, it has to meet the expectation of the reader in terms of matching the interior to the exterior. Secondly, it has to look professional. Thirdly, it needs to be adequately visible as a thumbprint-sized photograph on a website.

Try this experiment: open a browser and surf to your favorite online book retailer. Look up your favorite author and study the cover of their books. Consider how small the titles and name appears on the page. This is the reader's first look at your cover if they're browsing the online store.

It may be the only glance you get – so make it count.

Sure, once you have the reader's attention, they can be coerced into opening a sample, perhaps even downloading and reading a chapter or two. But in order to hook them, you've got to get them that far in the first place.

Today's book shopping experience is different. Embrace the change and make it work for you. There are a lot of ideas in the blogosphere about what constitutes quality and of course many people disagree. Read the suggestions and know what to avoid.

Learn to be discerning about cover design:

Book Cover Design for Indie Publishers
http://allindiepublishing.com/author-interviews/joel-friedlander-on-book-cover-design-for-indie-publishers/

Rethink Cover Design for a Small Small World
http://www.digitalbookworld.com/2013/thing-2-suggestive-seduction-and-the-naked-truth-rethink-cover-design-for-a-small-small-world/

Yes, We Really do Judge Books by Their Covers
http://www.huffingtonpost.com/2013/05/30/book-cover-design-indies_n_3354504.html

14 Tips for Good Kindle Cover Design
http://humblenations.com/2012/04/12/14-tips-for-good-kindle-cover-design/

The bottom line is you can hire someone to create a cover, make one yourself, or buy a readymade design. There are probably other ideas out there, but this pretty much encompasses the easiest approaches. First off, unless you are an experienced graphic designer with knowledge of book layout and design elements, don't take the do-it-yourself route. Please. I'll tell you why – the results are usually substandard and it cheapens your overall impact. Doing your own cover may be sufficient if you're doing a simple project for home consumption, but the minute you decide to market to others, you've raised the bar. Meet it.

Besides, acquiring a cover can be downright inexpensive.

I've tried all three approaches with varying degrees of success. Experience has taught me that expensive does not always equal quality and cheap is not necessarily synonymous with lousy. Many book cover designers create multiple mock-ups when a client orders an original design. Only one will be sold and the others are often dumped into the ready-made stock with sufficient changes to make them uniquely different from the original. Cover designers also practice their skills by trying out new designs with pre-made stock. This means you can buy a unique one-time cover for a fraction of the price of having one made.

Covers can cost thousands of dollars or be less than the cost of lunch at a family restaurant. Your choice. Money tendered for a quality cover is well spent. Like any other industry, you pay for name recognition. The first cover I purchased was designed by a well-known and established designer. I paid a premium price because I didn't know any better and I was nervous about the whole process. I'm pleased with the final result but even happier about my second cover which cost less than 10% of the first.

Some authors seem to feel the need to spend a lot of money to acquire the work of an established designer. I think they believe it adds cachet to their work. In the end, the only thing that matters – no matter how prettily the package is put together – is the quality of the story inside. Covers matter but not more than the writing.

My favorite book cover resources:

Go On Write
http://goonwrite.com/

Cheeky Covers
http://cheekycovers.com/

Wicked Smart Designs
http://www.wickedsmartdesigns.com/#!stock-covers/c1xmk

Quirky-Gurl Media
http://quirkygurl.com/cover-art/

Art by Karri
http://artbykarri.com/pre-made-covers/

Alchemy Bookcovers and Design
http://www.alchemybookcovers.com/#!premade-covers/cfvg

Dream Spring Pre-made Covers

http://marionsipe.blogspot.com/p/premade-book-covers-for-sale.html

Fantasia Frog Designs

http://fantasiafrogdesigns.wordpress.com/premade-bookcovers/

Spittyfish Designs

http://spittyfish.wordpress.com/designs-unclaimed/

There are several other things to keep in mind when you're shopping for a book cover. Make sure the cover you purchase is only being sold once. Some images are popular and since graphic designers source most of their materials from the same stock photo places, there is always the chance that you'll see part of your design on someone else's book. It happens. That's different than having the exact same cover appear on two different author's books – a situation much worse that showing up to a party wearing the same frock as the hostess.

Nobody wants that.

You also want to make sure that the person providing your book cover clarifies the licensing limits on the images for both digital and print purposes. Most images have limitations about how they can be used and how many times they can be reproduced (this includes print covers and promotional materials created to market that book). Usually the digital-use is unlimited and the print-use is curtailed. While most Indie authors will never hit the limits on these (especially for print editions), it is smart to know the maximums. Should you be lucky enough to run into that sort of problem, you can negotiate for a new license or simply have a new cover designed.

Premade book covers are an inexpensive solution but do be aware that if you plan to offer both a digital and print edition of your book – the covers require separate set-ups. It is possible to take a digital cover and turn it into a print one but the image has to be resized to fit properly and most of the time the clarity of the image is too small to provide a nice clear printed image. Many authors only publish digital editions but the additional expense for a print cover can often be rolled into the process as a package deal. I recommend offering a print edition simply because paperback books offer special opportunities that digital can't.

Each retailer where you make your book available will have a set structure and explicit guidelines for what they will accept. Unfortunately, they won't be the same. There is no industry standard, not even for the physical dimensions of an actual book. Here are a few informative links about the importance of pixels, image size and clarity, and the appropriate DPI for print and digital use in book covers:

Print and Ebook Covers, a Matter of Resolution
http://www.thebookdesigner.com/2012/01/print-and-e-book-covers-a-matter-of-resolution/

Ebook Cover File Size Specifications
http://www.thebookdesigner.com/2011/10/e-book-cover-file-size-specifications/

Ebook Specific Cover Design: Size and Resolution
http://www.digitalbookworld.com/2011/ebook-specific-cover-design-size-and-resolution/

PART FIVE

Print a Paperback

Printed books are like really large business cards that advertise for you.

❧

Whether or not you produce print books for each of your releases is a personal decision. I believe it's important to make the commitment. Print books travel. That should be reason enough. They wind up in boxes and on bookshelves; get left behind in airports and motels. With a printed copy of your book you have the potential to reach an entirely different audience by default. And, there's nothing like holding your own book between your moist little palms to remind you that you're really published.

Formatting a printed book is an entirely different experience. Hiring a professional book designer is a major expense, probably something you would undertake only if you were confident that you had an existing market that guaranteed sales – like a non-fiction release.

Other options include hiring out to a formatter (these work much cheaper than an actual interior designer) but results vary significantly. My first cover designer included basic formatting. I thought it looked stunning until I compared it to some of the novels in my home library.

The value of using templates:

In an effort to find a solution for producing a reasonably decent print book design, I discovered a professional book designer had already addressed the issue. Book templates are available through most of the publishing retailer sites but they are very simplistic. As the owner of The Marin Bookworks, as well as being a professional book designer himself, Joel Friedlander and his team have created a workable series of templates for use by Indie authors.

Huzzah!

Joel recognized that self-published books often lack the attention to detail that professionally designed books offer. Part of this is due to the tools at our disposal. Few people have the specialized programs to manipulate fine details in layout, and don't want to absorb the expense of buying software that has no other use. As a self-published author himself and the architect of The Book Designer blog (http://www.thebookdesigner.com/), Joel set out to develop templates that worked with Microsoft Word.

He succeeded.

This is no exaggeration; these are wonderful templates for use with both print and digital works. They look professional and are easy to use. The price is not prohibitive considering you can purchase a license for a single use, multiple uses, or even commercial quantities. Additionally, there are fiction and non-fiction templates and multiple styles to appeal to a wide range of preferences. Check out the nine current offerings at Book Design Templates (http://www.bookdesigntemplates.com/) and you won't be sorry.

Making print books work for you:

Print books are concrete objects that convince even the skeptics that you are serious about your publishing career. People who express amusement about your hobby suddenly change their tune when confronted with a printed copy of your work.

Consider all the ways you can utilize print books and think about how to turn them into tools for success.

I think of them as being oversized business cards that are handed around long after they leave my control. They provide endless advertising as they transfer from one reader to the next.

Print copies often generate opportunities by getting you invited to speaking engagements, readings at local coffee houses, and recognition in the local community. Printed books get accepted by libraries where they sit on shelves just waiting to be read. They also get borrowed and abandoned in empty lots – only to be rescued by a passerby. Books land in trashcans and hotel rooms – being picked up and discarded by countless hands. They get re-sold in rummage sales and covered in mildew spots, and go on to explore the world. They live multiple lives and touch dozens, perhaps hundreds of people. Even if you only want a single copy to sit above your desk, that book can be shown to others and admired by many.

There are numerous outlets that provide publishing services but unless you're confident about your ability to move a large number of volumes, stick to print-on-demand for your printed publishing needs. With POD technology you pay only for the copies you actually order and receive and don't end up with a huge overstock of printed copies you've paid for and now can't sell. Different retailers offer the ability to incorporate interior color inserts and images, different shades of white or cream paper for the pages, and even options about paperback and hardcover options.

Print book resources:

Createspace (paperback)
https://www.createspace.com/

Lightning Source (hardcover)
https://www1.lightningsource.com/default.aspx

Lulu (paperback and hardcover)
http://www.lulu.com/

PART SIX

Choose Distribution

Getting your book into the hands of readers is a challenging task.

❦

O ne of the biggest advantages traditional publishing offers, is access to the network of retailers and distribution lines that exists. This is one of the most difficult
aspects of the self-publishing approach. Access to retailers is
growing. The process of publication is being streamlined. The
market for digital books has increased at an accelerating rate
over the last five years and will likely continue to do so.

Selecting a retailer depends on how widespread you want distribution. At first, you might think the-wider-the-better and
that would be a logical choice. Like so many aspects of publishing, it depends on your goals and how much control you want to
maintain. Most of that has to do with marketing approaches.

While there are thousands of retail outlets where books are offered, only a handful are major players when it comes to moving inventory. Those are the ones to concentrate your efforts on if selling books is your goal. Some of these also offer distribution to outside outlets and then there are the actual distribution services. You have to decide which is best for you.

Distribution sources include:

Amazon's Kindle Direct Publishing
https://kdp.amazon.com/self-publishing/signin

Kobo's Writing Life
http://www.kobo.com/writinglife

Barnes & Noble's Nook Press
https://www.nookpress.com/

Apple's iBookstore
http://support.apple.com/kb/PH2808

Smashwords
http://www.smashwords.com/

Bookbaby
http://www.bookbaby.com/

eBook Partnership
http://www.ebookpartnership.com/

Vook
http://vook.com/

Amazon is the strongest bookseller in the self-publishing industry right now but many others offer great opportunities. The likelihood of a future shift is a given. There are differences in cost and benefits to each, so make sure you do your homework before jumping in feet first. For example, royalty rates vary depending on the outlet and the price of your book. At Amazon, the current rate is 70% for a book priced between 2.99 and 9.99 – while books priced lower earn a 35% royalty. At Barnes & Noble the royalty rates are 65% and 40% for similar price levels.

One of the great aspects of these distribution channels is they make your work available through their internal network. This means that your book gets offered for sale in every country serviced. Amazon sells your work in more than 100 countries. iBooks is catching up, making your work available in more than 50 countries.

That's global coverage.

Each retailer has their own quirks about what they think is okay and what is not. Read the details carefully. This is where a network of authors, social media connections, and colleagues are really helpful. If you don't know the specifics, there is always someone who can share their calamitous experience.

For example, if you publish through the iBooks store, Apple won't permit links to other retailers or mention of competitors. One of the big buttons Amazon has is not being undersold. If their bots find your book priced lower elsewhere, they'll undercut the price even if it means your book gets offered for FREE. Complain all you want, but those are the rules and they get to make them. Amazon's response will be too-bad-so-sad.

Examples like the Amazon one are the reason I don't use Smashwords. I know many people who use them and love them. One of their major detractions is they are notoriously slow to change prices. Since there is no way to confirm that the price of your book has been changed throughout their network of distributors, you can't argue the point if it comes up. This can be a costly situation if your book is selling well on Amazon and it gets price-matched to some remote distributor that never produces an income stream for you anyways and suddenly your book is being given away.

The great part about self-publishing is you control every aspect of the process from start to finish. You can change prices, put books on sale or take them off, run promotions, and even upload new versions if you find a typo or want to update content.

PART SEVEN

Price Strategically

Book prices are irrelevant – unless you're buying or selling.

❧

Some books sell in a high enough volume that low prices are productive. Many authors have found this to be a successful method of moving thousands of copies. Likewise, there is an endless influx of inexpensive and free books driving the enormous consumption. This strategy has driven some writers to list their book at .99 with the thought of making their work price-attractive to readers. You can read a metric ton of anecdotal evidence for why this is an awesome or a horrible idea – just pull up your favorite browser and start surfing.

Better yet, try it yourself and see what happens. The market is always in motion. What works one day, fails the next, and is reborn the following month. Experiment. You have control, exercise your abilities.

Many Indie authors tweak book prices as a part of their marketing strategy, with varying results. Some people believe that exposure will translate to sales in other ways.

For example, books that are listed at a higher price generally produce lower sales numbers but they offer a higher profit margin when listed at a cover price of 3.99 and up. Offering your book as a FREE download during a promotion through KDP Select (Amazon's exclusive program) or as a perma-FREE volume can be tremendously valuable. This is especially true if you're trying to reach new readers and sell additional volumes in a series. Again, you have to determine what your long-term approach necessitates.

Sites for figuring out pricing dynamics:

Power Pricing: How Should I Price My E-Books?
http://kobowritinglife.com/2012/12/11/power-pricing-how-should-i-price-my-ebooks/

Does Low-Balling Attract the Wrong Kind of Reader?
http://allindiepublishing.com/author-interviews/zoe-winters-on-ebook-pricing/

The New World of Publishing: Pricing Indie Books
http://www.deanwesleysmith.com/?p=6391

Ebook Pricing
http://jakonrath.blogspot.com/2010/09/ebook-pricing.html

Remember that even if you're just having fun and you plan to approach self-publishing as a hobby, you are still participating in a business-oriented industry. Be savvy. Be professional because you're playing on the same playground with a lot of very serious people. You may never become a best-selling writer but you will be a published author. You don't need to be an expert in everything but it helps to:

1. Make a business plan.
2. Create a marketing strategy.
3. Decide how to promote your books.

When it comes to determining a cover price, start with what seems like an appropriate dollar amount. Look at the competition. How are books – the ones similar to yours in length, style, and genre – being priced? Chances are, the numbers will be all over the place, so you'll still have to take a stab at it and try out a few different price points.

Despite the argument that some pundits posit, that ebooks should be cheaper than print because the overhead is only a fraction of the expense, digital publishing still incurs costs. Some of them can be steep. Granted, it isn't the expense of traditional print runs for paperbacks, but the dollars can still add up. When you're the publisher as well as the writer, then the cost of editing and proofreading also gets rolled into that total.

The bottom line on pricing:

Don't offer your book at a lower price than you feel comfortable putting it out there. Experiment and re-evaluate over time. Manipulate the retail situation until you're happy with the results. Offer marketing and promotion to keep your book higher in the rankings. The more visibility you can achieve, the better success you'll see. Some books sit on market and do virtually nothing – then skyrocket over night for no apparent reason. Generally, the buzz has been building. One person has read the book and recommended it to another. The process snowballs and suddenly there's a jump in sales.

Sometimes it never happens.

Anecdotal input suggests that the more works an author has on market, the greater the likelihood for upward movement. This makes sense for readers who find an author they like and want to read everything they have available.

Don't rush.

Publishing is changing but the landscape is going to be wide open for years to come. If anything, we'll see an increase in opportunity as more platforms come online and competition grows.

PART EIGHT

Market & Promote

Word of mouth remains the best sales method – buzz sells books.

❧

Without doubt, getting self-published books into the hands (virtual and otherwise) of readers remains the greatest challenge. There has been an escalation of venues created in order to do just this, but sometimes getting your foot in the door is rough. Competition is huge. The sheer volume of work being funneled through retailers is a deterrent. Your book gets lost in the shuffle. The best way to get seen is to reach the top of the popularity list and that takes work and sometimes, luck.

A great thing about being a writer is that readers consume faster than authors can produce new material. There is no real competition over readers although some writers act very territorial. It isn't necessary. Readers will outstrip our ability to produce, every time.

Marketing methods and promotional efforts create controversy. Nobody wants to be on the receiving end of the hard sell. The sleazy come-on is a turn-off. The last thing you want to experience is feeling like you just got side-swiped by the obligatory buy-me-read-me chant. It feels worse than when your colleagues hit you up to purchase their kids' Girl Scout cookies or school-fundraising wrapping paper. Self-published authors often resort to questionable tactics because they don't know any better. Marketing professionals offer well-intended advice that is fantastic to sell widgets – but pisses off readers no end. Selling books takes tact.

What works for one author may not work for another. Depending on your book, the market, the competition, and the potential reader who is attracted to your work, this is not a one-size-fits-all aspect of the adventure.

Finding traction in a crowded market:

Since there's already a tremendous volume of resources about how to market, and different types of promotional methods, here are some links you can browse. Harvest things that have potential for your situation and keep searching – this is an area of potentially unlimited growth.

A Checklist for Marketing Your E-Book
http://writerunboxed.com/2011/09/23/a-checklist-for-marketing-your-e-book/

How Readers Discovered a Debut Novel
http://www.goodreads.com/blog/show/394-how-readers-discovered-a-debut-novel-a-case-study

3 Keys to Successful and Sustainable Indie Authorship
http://janefriedman.com/2011/10/07/scott-sigler/

Amazon KDP Select: Is It Worthwhile for Authors?
http://janefriedman.com/2013/04/02/amazon-kdp-select/

Book Promotion: What's Working at Amazon in 2013?
http://www.lindsayburoker.com/amazon-kindle-sales/book-promotion-whats-working-at-amazon/

Maximizing Digital Sales
http://www.digitalbookworld.com/2011/maximizing-digital-book-sales/

How to Get Reviews for Self-Published Books
http://www.writersdigest.com/editor-blogs/there-are-no-rules/marketing-self-promotion/how-to-get-reviews-for-self-published-books

10 Ways to Find Reviewers for Your Self-Published Book
http://www.emptymirrorbooks.com/publishing/10-ways-to-find-reviewers-for-your-self-published-book.html

The Indie Reviewers List
http://www.theindieview.com/indie-reviewers/

How to Sell Self-Published Books: One at a Time
http://catherineryanhoward.com/2012/05/07/how-to-sell-self-published-books-one-at-a-time/

89 Book Marketing Ideas
http://www.authormedia.com/89-book-marketing-ideas-that-will-change-your-life/

Marketing Your Book
http://www.thebookdesigner.com/marketing-your-book/

Finding your niche in the market:

There's much to consider when it comes to marketing and promotion. Are you going to try and put your book in local book stores? Do you want your work in libraries? Will you hand sell to potential readers at readings and signings? Figuring out your path is tricky because it involves individual comfort levels. Once you figure out what might be a natural fit for your personality, then you have to determine what sort of opportunities exist and begin mining them for sales.

Search the web for sites that host short-term promotions, like when you offer your book for a reduced price. Some sites offer price categories for hosting your work in long-term and permanent situations – just look carefully at what you get in exchange for the cost.

Discount marketing your book:

Some of the best sites are those that revolve around mailing lists. Sites like BookBub (http://home.bookbub.com/home/) send emails to registered readers who indicate their reading preferences and receive a list of free or reduced-priced books in their mailbox every day. For writers, BookBub can be lucrative but it is costly. Their guidelines are also strict and they turn down a lot of self-published work based on quality and appeal. Since they offer the books of both traditional and Indie authors, if your work is selected, you can be in illustrious company. Name recognition is a huge advantage.

The importance of reviews:

Story Cartel (http://storycartel.com/) offers a different approach. They provide a free digital copy of your book to registered readers in exchange for an honest review. The only cost to the author is offering five print copies of your book as rewards for selected reviewers. If you don't offer your book in print, then you can still use this service by offering Amazon giftcards. Another aspect of Story Cartel which is really useful is that you get a copy of the email address for all the registered participants who downloaded your book. You want these for your mailing list because they've already indicated an interest in your work (hopefully not just that it was free). The plus side to a service like Story Cartel is getting more reviews on your work. The downside is receiving reviews from readers who only read your work because it was free and would otherwise have passed it by because it's not the kind of story that appeals to them. Bummer.

Reviews sell books.

It doesn't matter if the critiques are good or bad – but good always makes you feel better. Remember that reviews are for readers, not authors. People are entitled to their opinion and not everyone is going to like your work. That's okay. Sometimes a poorly rated review says the nicest things about you as an author. Pushing buttons at both ends of the rating spectrum means people are vested in your work.

Marketing and promotion often features that sort of trade-off, which is why it's important to find the approach that best works for you. Remember, be honest in the reviews you leave for others.

Never respond to negativity. Ever.

Always be professional.

Engage with the reading community:

A final note about exposure, involves a site called Goodreads (http://www.goodreads.com/). This website is geared toward readers. As an author, this is your dedicated audience – people who want to read. This is an active environment.

Additionally, Goodreads offers some really great opportunities for authors. Not only do authors get special access and services, they also can make use of numerous promotional methods – all of which are FREE. As a Goodreads author, you are in the company of well-known and unknown colleagues. You can host events and invite participants to join you. You can recommend books to followers (not just your own). There are groups you can belong to, organize, and create. Self-service advertising puts your book cover out there with a brief description for a minor cost. I've had over half a million views of two books and I still haven't used up the initial seventy-five dollar investment. If you have print copies of your books, you can offer giveaways and create interest and buzz in your new releases, both before and after the actual event. You can recommend your book or any other to followers and, since Goodreads is also a social networking site, you can interact with millions of other users.

For real.

People will tell you it is impossible to become a best-selling author if you self-publish. They're wrong. Check out the Indie Bestseller List to see people break through the glass ceiling every month (http://www.indiebound.org/indie-bestsellers).

PART NINE

ISBNs & Copyright

Always use protection.

❧

Most of us know what ISBN numbers are, we've seen them on virtually every book we've ever read. But really, few people actually know what they do. So, what do they do? Well, they classify and categorize a book into a major system of organization. The acronym stands for international standard book identifier. This number makes sure that your book is linked to the correct information distributed to book sellers and readers.

In the United States, ISBNs are issued through a company called Bowker (https://www.myidentifiers.com/isbn/main). As the official ISBN agency of the U.S. these folks issue the numbers through their identifier services. Each country has their own portal for accessing and acquiring indentifiers. Once an identifier is used, it cannot be transferred to a new work. It's a one-time deal. As a publisher you open an account, log in the pertinent information for each identifier and it gets disseminated through the network. In the U.S. we pay a fee for this service and it can be substantial.

Do I have to get an ISBN#?

No – but you want one anyways.

You should get one for each book you publish. In fact, every format of your book needs its own ISBN number. This can add considerably to the expenses of producing work unless you take the plunge and buy in bulk. Consider this a necessary operating expense because it ensures your book remains yours and not the property of the publishing house you publish it through. For instance, you can publish your work without an ISBN but an identifier code of some sort will be assigned when you publish through a retailer. Each retailer will assign their own – thus making it impossible for your work to be tracked through the international system.

Current pricing options for ISBN#s:

A single ISBN is $125
A 10-pack of ISBNs is $250
A 100-pack of ISBNs is $575
A 1000-pack ISBNs is $1000

As you can see, buying in bulk makes sense, especially if you plan to release more than a single work. If you offer your novel as a digital copy, a paperback, a hardcover, and an audiobook – that's equal to four ISBN#s. They add up quick. Bowker will intimate that you need a separate identifier for each format of a digital book but as of right now, there is no way to archive and market individual formats. Additionally, with conversion sites on the internet, people can buy a single format and translate it into as many formats as they desire.

The Bowker website offers a lot of information about publishing and the importance of using the system to your benefit. It's worth spending some time studying the materials. Don't waste your money buying a barcode – online retailers provide them without cost (handy websites also offer the service FREE). Bowker does offer a couple of useful guides – these are worth downloading and saving to your files for future reference:

ISBN Guides: Basic Information
https://www.myidentifiers.com/sites/default/files/images/MYID +Basic+Information.pdf

Title Set-up & Registration
https://www.myidentifiers.com/sites/default/files/images/Title_ setup_and_registration.pdf

Do I need to copyright my book?

No – but you should do so anyways.

Everything we write is copyrighted by default but should you ever find yourself in a position where you must prove the work is yours, then copyright is essential. The legal world is filled with anecdotes of people who lost court cases where they were clearly the rightful owner of a work but because they had never officially copyrighted the material in question, they could not prove it in the eyes of the law.

Protect yourself by registering the copyright on your book. If you remember to do this after you release the digital format, you can literally upload your samples copy. If you choose only to offer print copies then you have to pony up a book to them for record-keeping. Don't pay an intermediary to do this - the cost runs $35 and can be done directly through the copyright office (http://www.copyright.gov/help/faq/faq-register.html).

This is inexpensive insurance if you ever need to prove the book in question is yours. While this seems an outlandish idea, digital publishing has made piracy an entire new industry.

Should I use digital rights management?

Piracy has raised concerns about how to protect electronic intellectual property. Digital Rights Management (DRM) is one solution. You have to make your own decision regarding this issue but I don't bother with it. There are websites dedicated to stripping DRM out of locked formats and off secured devices. People will find a way to pirate your work. I prefer to believe in the basic honesty and goodness of the public. Sure, there will be people who steal it, but they aren't likely to have been the folks who might have bought it in the first place.

If it makes you feel better, use it. Book retailers offer an option when you first put your book up for sale and you can always edit to make changes at any time.

PART TEN

Collect Resources

Build yourself a library of go-to industry experts.

❧

W hat works for one writer doesn't always fit the bill for another when it comes to publishing. Only we know what our ultimate goals include and sometimes those don't become clear until we've been floundering around for a time. Make use of the information that fits your needs and let the rest of it go. If something doesn't ring true for you, keep searching for the method or formula that makes the most sense. If it feels wrong – don't do it. If it seems overly simplistic – it might just be. As with any endeavor, success and failure is measured in minute portions until we learn our way.

Publishing is no different.

Read blogs, make lists, collate expert input, experiment with your own work. Draw conclusions. Share information. The online writing community offers generous feedback and friend-ships – you can connect with people who are seasoned and expe-rienced in both the traditional and Indie publishing worlds. Send an email, connect with a tweet, put yourself out there where readers can find you. If you don't, how will you ever ar-rive at your destination on the best-seller lists?

Don't forget to reach out with questions.

You can always contact me and if I don't know, I bet we can find the answer with a little research and some networking. Writing is a solitary endeavor but publishing is more like a team event. You can go it alone but only if you want it to be that way. There are many routes to publication – find the one that works for you and give it a shot.

Really, what have you got to lose?

ABOUT THE AUTHOR

As an anthropologist, Lesann divides her time between academic interests and professional research. Focused primarily on the American west, she is inspired by the geologic features of empty landscapes. The ancient art and prehistory of those settings often feature in her work. She writes about messed-up people and sinister events, saying her stories often feature paranormal or romantic elements because life is boring without spooky stuff and warm bodies. Crossing genre lines, she pens both contemporary and historical mysteries, romantic suspense, and even a little horror.

Visit WWW.LESANNBERRY.COM for new releases.

www.ingramcontent.com/pod-product-compliance
Lightning Source LLC
Chambersburg PA
CBHW060644280326
41933CB00012B/2145